# Annamaria Giusti

# STRASBOURG

## 81 COLOR ILLUSTRATIONS

ƎB
Bonechi Publisher

# INDEX

ISBN 88-7009-122-8

Credits:
*Photos by NORSTAIR:* Pages 1-3-5-7-21-24 (below)- 25-26-27-28-29-30-31-53.
*Photos by MARASCO:* Pages 20-22-23-24 (above).

*Translated by*
MERRY ORLING

© Copyright 1980 by
CASA EDITRICE BONECHI
Via dei Cairoli 18/b – Firenze
Telex 571323 CEB

Aerial view of the city.

# A BRIEF HISTORY

*Thanks to a favorable geographical position at the crossroads of waterways and overland routes, the territory on which present-day Strasbourg rises has been inhabited since the Bronze Age. At the time of the Roman conquest in 12 BC, the settlement, known as Argentoratum, became important mainly as a military outpost from which the outlying areas of the empire could be defended from the Germanic tribes not yet under Roman dominion.*

*After a period of obscurity following the fall of the Roman Empire, the town, now known as Stratisburgum, was rebuilt over its own ruins and,*

*during the Carolingian period, actually achieved considerable importance. However, its real economic and political growth began about 1100 with the rise of an enterprising middle class.*

*In 1262 the town was able to wrest itself free of the control of the bishops who, from the outset of the Middle Ages, had been the city's supreme, political authorities.*

*Strasbourg's population and territory expanded in step with its growing prosperity. In the second half of the 14th century, the Rhine was spanned with a great bridge. This put Strasbourg at the* crossroads of the trade routes of northern Europe. Duties on timber, wine, cotton, cloth, livestock, and fish were paid at its thriving customs house, in which produce and manufactured goods were sorted out on their way to the markets.

In order to secure the support of a city of such strategic economic importance, the emperors granted it numerous privileges and tax exemptions with the result that Strasbourg became more and more self-sufficient. Finally, in the 15th century, it became a free republic governed by a council made up of representatives of the guilds. The prosperity of Strasbourg continued to grow in the 16th century. One of the first cities to support the Protestant Reformation, it soon became one of its hotbeds, due to the presence of numerous reform thinkers, preachers, and steady streams of Swiss, Italian, and French refugees who, granted asylum in the city, greatly enriched its cultural life.

Towards the end of the 16th century, fierce internecine struggles within the city and warring among the major powers of north-central Europe brought about the city's political decline. The end result was the annexation of the Republic of Strasbourg to France in 1697. Nevertheless, the new close ties with France led to renewed prosperity and a renewed vigor in the city's cultural and social life.

The political events of the 18th and 19th centuries, starting with the French revolution, Napoleon, the Restoration and the Second Empire of Napoleon III, deeply affected Strasbourg as they did all of France. (The defeat of Napoleon III, for example, had especially grave consequences for the city.)

In 1870 after six weeks of bombing (which caused the destruction of a large part of the city, including its monuments), Strasbourg was annexed to the newly-formed German empire as the capital of the Alsace-Lorraine region.

Not until after World War I, in 1918, was she restored to France to whom, in truth, she had never spiritually ceased to belong. World War II brought new suffering, starting in 1940 with the brutal occupation by the Germans and their aggressive policy of Germanization, and ending with the allied bombing of the city in August and September 1944, a tragic error which caused numerous victims and widespread destruction.

In the post-war period Strasbourg has once more achieved the status of a European center, although this time in an entirely different way. In 1949 the city was picked to be the headquarters of the Council of Europe and since 1979 has been the seat of the 9-member European Parliament.

**The Cathedral viewed from above.**

# THE CATHEDRAL

The Cathedral de Nôtre-Dame "le grand Ange rose de Strasbourg," as Paul Claudel poetically described it, is one of the most incredible Gothic buildings in Northern Europe, even in comparison to its best-known French and German counterparts. The huge rosy-hued structure, rendered almost dainty by a complicated web of pinnacles and spires, dwarfs everything around it in the old city center. Here, at the edge of the Roman outpost, right over the ruins of a temple to Mars, once stood a late 6th century church dedicated to the Virgin. In the Carolingian period, according to a brief description left by the poet Ermoldus the Black in 826, the original building was enlarged, decorated, and a crypt commissioned by Archbishop Remy was added on.

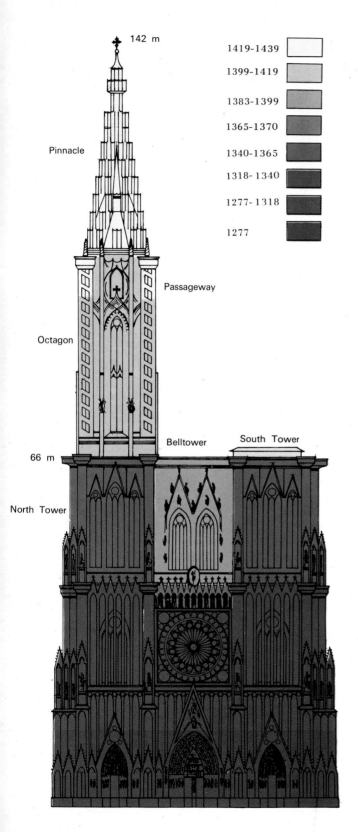

142 m

Pinnacle

Passageway

Octagon

Belltower    South Tower

66 m

North Tower

Unfortunately, the first cathedral was burned down in a fire set by the troops of the Duke of Sweden. An imposing Romanesque basilica founded in 1015 by Bishop Wernher of Hapsbourg was erected in its place. The size of this second church, completed in the mid 11th century, was truly impressive, if one considers that the present-day cathedral rises over its foundations.

It had single aisles ending in great transepts that opened directly into a semicircular apse flanked by chapels and surmounted by a sturdy tower. Throughout the 12th century its inner structures, mostly made of wood, were badly gutted in fires which broke out several times. Then, in 1176, Bishop Conrad of Hüneburg ordered the rebuilding of the east end so that the apse and crossing could be enlarged.

The result is an impressive example of the late Romanesque style, already tending to Gothic in the vertical thrust of the vaulting in the north transept. The south transept is even more Gothic, especially its densely-sculpted façade whose clear Ile-de-France influence reveals that Strasbourg was the first center of the Renan region to have picked up this advanced style.

Relations with France intensified during the bishopric of Berthold de Teck, Bishop of Strasbourg between 1223 and 1244. Owing to his strong ties with the French clergy, de Teck was well-informed on the development of the Gothic style in the cathedrals in Northern France, especially in the Paris area. In fact, it was under de Teck that the sculptor of the south portal and architect of the nave, both French, were summoned to work on the cathedral. Construction on the nave, begun in 1235, went on for forty years. It is a splendid example of the pure Gothic style, with soaring pointed arches that rest upon slender composite pillars and frame a procession of lusciously-colored stained glass windows. Practically two hundred years after work was begun, the cathedral could almost be considered complete when, in 1365, the main façade, flanked on either side by a belltower, was finished.

The majestic carved spire built on top of the south belltower between 1399 and 1439 was a fitting crowning touch. All the other projects carried out over the centuries to preserve and enhance the building are living proof of Strasbourg's great fondness for her cathedral, undoubtedly the best-loved monument in the whole city.

**The Cathedral and city viewed from above.** ▶

# THE FAÇADE

The façade is best approached from Rue Mercière, a medieval street lined with picturesque buildings. Rising at the end, as if a giant illustration from a Strasbourg history book had miraculously come to life, is the cathedral's breathtaking façade, its elaborate portal topped by the great rose window. Huge as it is, its harmonious proportions, intense vertical thrust, and the complex light and shade patterns created by an intricate web of sculptural decoration, somehow give it the appearance of being incredibly light and delicate.

$214^1/_2$ feet high and 146 feet wide, the façade was built between 1277 and 1365 and completed when the pinnacle, designed by Ulrich of Ensingen, architect of the cathedral of Ulma, was raised in the early 1500s, thus extending its total height to 461 feet. The original façade design, attributed to a legendary figure, Erwin of Steibach, underwent various changes throughout the almost 100-year-period it took to built it. This is thoroughly documented by numerous contemporary drawings preserved in the Nôtre-Dame Cathedral Museum.

The remarkable sculptural decoration, clustered mainly around the three portals, was damaged several times during the Reformation and Revolutionary periods. As a result, in the late 19th-early 20th centuries some of the sculptures had to be restored, while still others had to be taken down and replaced by copies (the originals are preserved in the Cathedral Museum).

The complex iconographic scheme of the façade sculpture starts out on the left portal with *scenes from the childhood of*

◀ The Cathedral and Rue Mercière.

The Cathedral – The central portal of the west side. ▶

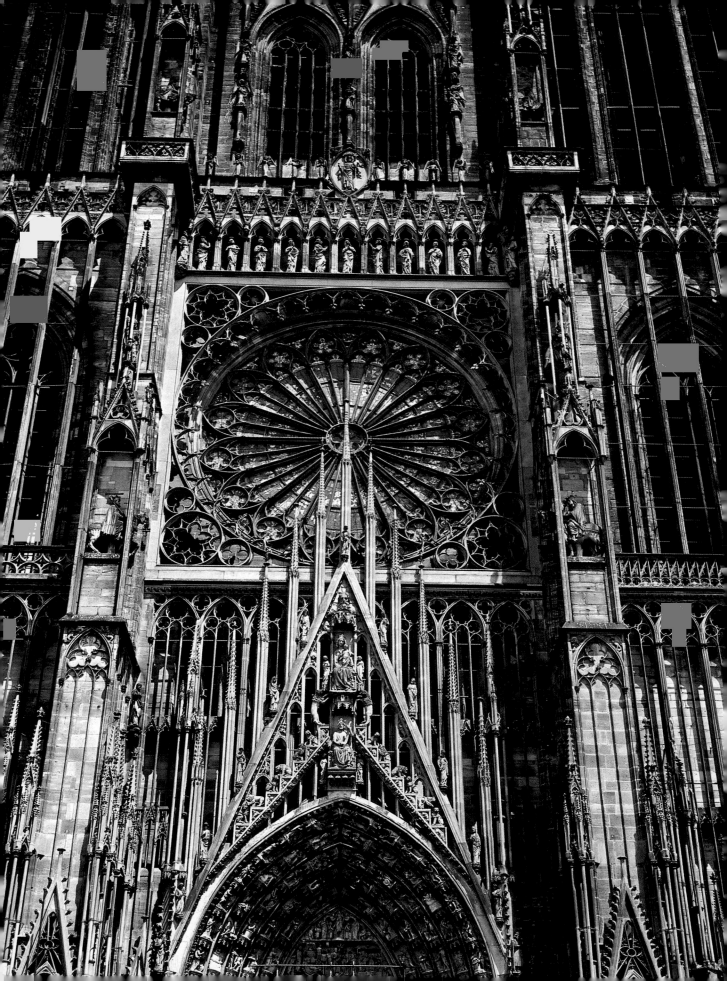

*Christ* in the tympanum and *personifications of Virtues slaying vices* on the jambs. The jamb statues of the central portal represent *prophets* with the *Virgin and Child* in the middle. The four registers of the tympanum recount *stories of the Passion,* culminating in the *Crucifixion of Christ.* Above, in the triangular-shaped gable, are twelve lions symbolizing the 12 tribes of Israel and seated statues of Solomon (below) and the Virgin (above). The scene in the tympanum of the righthand portal shows the *Last Judgment* with the *Wise Virgins being greeted by their betrothed and the Foolish Virgins being tempted into sin.*

This project was entirely carried out in the last quarter of the 13th century. The style of the carvings was to a great extent influenced by the refined Gothic sculpture popular in Paris in the mid 1200s, but as a result of strong local Alsatian and Renan influxes, they reveal personal touches of expressiveness rarely found in their Parisian counterparts. Each of the three portals reflects the style peculiar to the group of artists who worked on it: while the righthand one reveals the overriding influence of popular art, the middle one is much more sophisticated, and the lefthand one is wholly centered upon the dramatic effect of the subject.

Above the central portal is the embroidery-like rose window over which runs a delicate loggia with figures of apostles and equestrian statues of Merovingian and Carolingian kings (19th century restorations).

The upper section of the façade is characterized by pairs of three-part mullioned windows.

The Cathedral  The tympanum and rose-window over the entranceway.

The Cathedral – The elaborate sculptural decoration of the entranceway. ▶

The Cathedral – Portal: the Devil and the Foolish Virgins.

The Cathedral – Portal: Christ and the Wise Virgins.

## Buttresses and spires

A complex system of flying buttresses along the outside of the building makes it possible to achieve the upward thrust of the nave. Most of the statues decorating the spires and pinnacles along the sides, except for those on the eastern buttresses, are 19th century creations. Those on the east side were sculpted around 1240-1250 by the same artists active in the south transept. At the turn of the 14th century it was decided that the proper crowning touch to the cathedral would be a soaring spire to rise over the lefthand façade belltower. The ambitious project was undertaken by the architect Ulma Ulrich of Ensingen who erected the spire's massive eight-sided base and the four little turrets on each side housing the service staircases. Upon Ulrich's death, the project was taken up by Jean Hultz of Cologne who built the pyramid-shaped spire which has little carved pinnacles coming out of it like little flames.

Reaching a total height of $461^{1}/_{2}$ feet, the spire made the Cathedral of Strasbourg, up until the 19th century, the tallest building in the western world. Although no longer a record-holder, it will always remain one of the most incredible achievements of the skill and daring of the Gothic architects.

◀ The Cathedral – Detail of the statues along the side of the building.

◀ The Cathedral – The buttresses.

The Cathedral – The pinnacle. ▶

The Cathedral – View of the Saint-Laurent Portal.

## The Saint-Laurent Portal

Despite the fact that the cathedral was practically completed by the second half of the 1300s, countless projects to further embellish it were undertaken throughout the centuries.

One of the most important of these is the chapel of Saint-Laurent (St. Lawrence), now used as the sacristy, which was added on to the façade of the south transept between 1495 and 1505. Designed by Jacques de Landsuth, it is a first rate example of the elaborate style known as Flamboyant Gothic. Above the entrance is a huge baldachino encrusted with garlands framing a *scene of the martyrdom of St. Lawrence*. On the jambs are statues, one of *St. Lawrence* and the other of *the Virgin and Child*.

On either side are pinnacles, so finely-carved they look as though a goldsmith had chiselled them. They are adorned with animated figures of the *three Magi* on the left and *Sts. Gregory, Vincent, James, and Maurice* on the right, all by Jean of Aix-la-Chapelle.

16

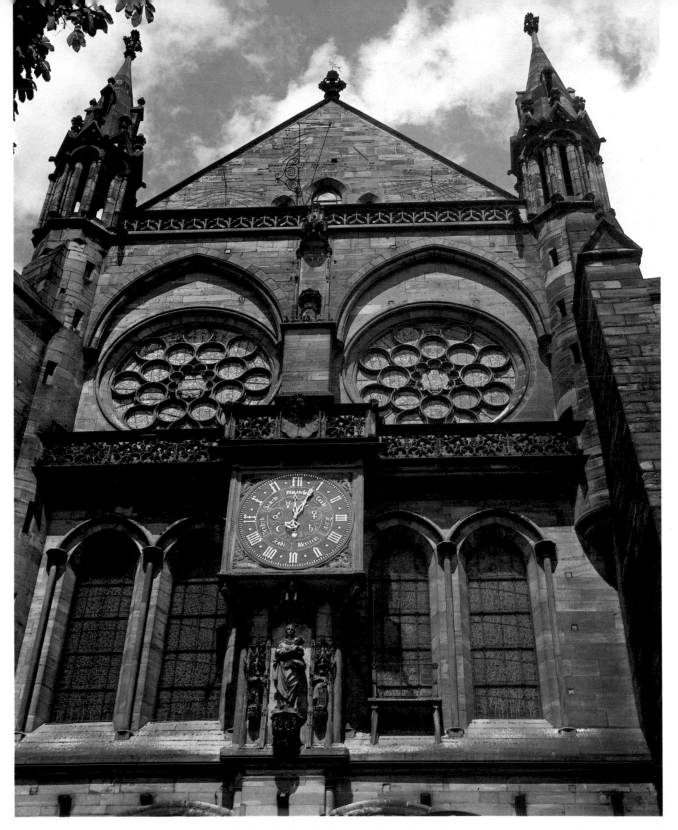

The Cathedral – Detail of the façade of the south transept.

## Portal of the south transept

The double portal leading to the south transept, though Romanesque in style, is decorated with remarkable Gothic reliefs and statues, which rank amongst the cathedral's highlights. The large female jamb statues on either side (copies, the originals are displayed in the Cathedral Museum), are allegorical figures. The delicately-curved one on the right, blindfolded, symbolizes the *Synagogue,* while the one on the left a more solemn, forceful figure, represents the *Church Triumphant.* In the portal lunettes are equally remarkable reliefs, depicting the *Coronation and Death of the Virgin.* The vigorous treatment of the drapery and animated poses of the figures create an effect of subtle emotivity. The seated *statues of Solomon* and the *Virgin* above are 19th century imitation-Gothic additions. Above the portal is the outer face of the astronomical clock located inside the transept.

The Cathedral – Portal
of the south transept.

The Cathedral – Portal of the south transept: Personification of the Synagogue.

The Cathedral – Portal of the south transept: Personification of the Church.

### The interior

For its day, the huge nave — built in 39 years from 1236 to 1275 — was put up in no time. One of the most remarkable and perfect examples of the High Gothic style, it was designed by a masterful but unknown architect, who achieved a free interpretation and, at the same time, fusion, of elements typical of the great Gothic cathedrals of the Ile-de-France, Champagne, and Bourgogne regions. In fact, in the nave, composite pillars, three-part windows, pointed arches, and capitals combine to create a dynamic architectural masterpiece beautifully highlighted in the glow of the rosy-hued stone and the stained glass. The construction of the nave began at the apse end and continued westward following the perimeter of the pre-existing Romanesque basilica. This is why the aisles are so wide— unlike those of most Gothic churches— and explains the unusual 1:2 ratio of width to height which, in comparison to the other Gothic cathedrals of Northern France, reduces the effect of overall verticality.

The Cathedral – The pulpit.

## The pulpit

About halfway along the nave is a sculpted pulpit, so finely carved it looks like a piece of jewelry a hundred times enlarged. It was built expressly for a preacher, Geiler of Kayserberg, in 1484-1485. The statuettes in the middle represent the *Virgin between Sts. Barbara and Catherine, with Sts. Moses, Jerome, and Pope Leo IX*. In the upper section is an expressive *Crucifixion*, while the sides are adorned with statues of eight apostles and angels bearing the instruments of their martyrdom.

The little dog, curled up asleep at the foot of the railing is one of the charming naturalistic touches the Northern sculptors of the period were so fond of. According to a popular tradition, it is a portrait of a dog once owned by Reverend Geiler which, during his master's interminable sermons, would curl up for a nice long nap.

## The apse

The present-day cathedral was started in the 12th century from the apse end over the foundations of the earlier Romanesque basilica. In fact, the great convexity of the apse and the splayed arches supporting it, which create the illusion of an ambulatory, are still very Romanesque in style. The great stained glass window with the *Virgin protectress of the city, surrounded by doves,* is a modern work by Max Ingrand. It was donated to the cathedral in 1956 by the member countries of the European Council. The painted ceiling, dating from the 19th century, is meant to imitate Byzantine mosaics. Beneath the slightly raised apse is a three-part crypt, adorned with friezes and carved capitals. This is all that remains of the Romanesque church destroyed in the 12th century by fire.

## The organ

By the nave entrance is an elaborate organ built by Frederic Krebs at the end of the 15th century and altered by André Silvermann in the early 1700s. Its sumptuous carved wooden case dates from 1385. The bearded figure astride a lion at the pointed base represents *Samson*. On either side are bearded figures carved out of wood. The one on the left represents a guardsman playing a trumpet, while the long-haired figure on the right has always been known as Rohraffe.
The figures are actually giant marionettes whose heads, arms, and mouths used to be operated by a person sitting inside a little cabin in the middle, who was also Rohraffe's voice. One of Rohraffe's favorite pastimes was making fun of preachers, which he often did quite cuttingly. In fact, the illustrious

The Cathedral – The great rose-window of the façade.

preacher Geiler of Kaiserberg once actually brought the matter to court, although the presiding judge failed to give him satisfaction.

## The stained glass windows

In the words of Paul Claudel, the cathedral of Strasbourg, *"reconte à travers les vitraux tous les siècles, toute l'histoire profane et sacrée"* (through the windows, all the centuries and the entire stream of sacred and profane history are recounted). Indeed, the stained glass windows throughout the church — in the nave, transepts, chapels, and crypt — are closely tied in with the building's long history, creating an exquisite complement to the architecture and sculptural decoration.

The Cathedral – Stained glass windows of the crypt.

In keeping with the tradition of the Gothic cathedrals of France, huge rose windows pierce the main façade and transept ends. The transept windows with *Old Testament scenes* are the oldest, having been executed in the early 13th century in the Byzantine style. The great rose window of the façade 45$^1/_2$ feet in diameter, was inspired by the one above the north portal of Nôtre-Dame in Paris, but the original mid 14th century panes were restored in 1845. The subjects of the nave and transept windows, executed by various workshops between the 13th and 14th centuries, are *Old and New Testament scenes* interspersed with

The Cathedral – Some of the stained glass windows.

The Cathedral – Relief showing the Garden of Gethsemane.

*figures of saints, martyrs, and emperors.* Together they form a complex *summa* of the religious and civic history of the city. In the crypt, the only part of the Romanesque cathedral still extant, is the cathedral's oldest surviving window (12th century), with a hieratic frontal figure representing an archangel.

## The Garden of Gethsemane and the carved wooden altars

Over the centuries the cathedral became a living museum of the arts and crafts, not only of the city, but of the entire region as well. This, to a great extent, came about as treasures destined for other churches found their way to the Strasbourg cathedral. Noteworthy examples are the 13th and 14th centuries stained glass windows in the Chapel of Saint-Laurent, originally executed for a Dominican church and the sculpture group depicting Christ's Sermon in the Garden of Gethsemane, displayed as a kind of sacred representation, in the north transept. Sculpted by Veit Wagner in 1498 for the cemetery of the church of St. Thomas, the statues were brought to the cathedral in 1667. Also, the two 16th century carved wooden altars placed on either side of the stairs leading up to the choir were originally executed for other churches. The one on the left, the *Altar of Saint-Pancrace,* from Dangolsheim, is a triptych with wings and shows *St. Pancras dressed in princely robes between Sts. Catherine and Nicholas.* The panel reliefs portray the *Nativity* and the *Adoration of the Magi,* On the back are four figures of saints, visible, naturally, only when the panels are shut. The altar on the right, also a triptych, shows *St. Maurice between Sts. Nicholas, Roch, Matthew, and Florian.* Although the craftsmanship is not quite as refined as that of its counterpart, this altar is nevertheless an especially fine example of the vigorous, more folky style which was widespread throughout Northern Europe during the Middle Ages.

26

The Cathedral –
Triptych depicting
St. Maurice with
Sts. Nicholas, Roch.
Matthew, and
Florian.

The Cathedral –
Altar depicting
St. Pancras with
Sts. Catherine and
Nicholas; on the
sides, the Nativity
and the Adoration
of the Magi.

## The Angel Pillar

The Angel Pillar, more properly the Last Judgment Pillar, is located in the center of the south transept. Not only a highlight of the cathedral itself, this sculpture ranks as one of the masterpieces of High Gothic sculpture in its peak period.

The earlier massive pillar supporting the vault of the north transept has here been transformed into a slender cluster of eight columns with three registers of statuary. The lower one is adorned with the *four Evangelists* identified by their symbols, the middle one with *four angels blowing trumpets,* and the upper one with *Christ enthroned amidst angels holding symbols of the Passion.* Executed c. 1235-1245 by an unknown artist dubbed "the first among the Gothic masters," these exquisite carvings are a notable reflection of the sculptural style then dominant in the great French Gothic cathedrals such as Chartres.

## The astronomical clock

The astronomical clock located in the south transept cannot be considered just a curiosity that has amazed hundreds and thousands of people over the centuries, for nothing more than this 16th century marvel embodies the spirit of the Renaissance and its unique combination of science, technology, and art. Made to replace a 14th century clock, it was begun in 1547, left unfinished, and finally completed between 1571 and 1574. It required a team of artists and scientists: a mathematician

The Cathedral –
The Angel Pillar.

The Cathedral –
View of the
astronomical clock.

(Dasypodius), watchmakers (the Habrecht brothers), an architect (Hans Uhlberger, who built its elaborate wooden housing), and a painter (Tobie Stimmer, who decorated it and prepared the models for the sculptures). Later, from 1838 to 1842, J. B. Schwilgué was commissioned to restore the complicated works which provide various astronomical indications. What people come to see, however, are the delightful wooden figures that mark the hours. Every sixty minutes Christ comes out to chase Death, portrayed as a skeleton, who is allowed to strike his fatal blows only on the hour. Every quarter of an hour, four male figures, representing the four ages of man, ring bells. At noon the apostles pass before Christ, bow their heads to receive his blessing while, at the same time, a rooster spreads his wings and crows. Before re-entering, Christ turns toward the assembled crowd and makes a blessing, and the charming scene is over.

The Cathedral – The astronomical clock: in the photo above, detail of Christ blessing and below, the Ages of Man passing in front of Death.

The Cathedral – The astronomical clock: in the center photo: the carts symbolizing the days of the week.

The Cathedral – The astronomical clock: in the photo below, the Heavenly Globe and, in the background, the perpetual calendar with statues of Diana and Apollo.

# THE LITTLE CATHEDRAL MUSEUM

A small but fascinating museum has been set up in an 18th century gallery, built on the site of a cloister demolished in the 16th century, and which is connected to the cathedral. The exhibits include fragments of sculpture from the cathedral exterior, wrought-iron rood screens, and stained glass windows. The highlight is a remarkable set of *fourteen tapestries with scenes of the life of the Virgin,* woven between 1638 to 1657 for the choir of the Cathedral of Paris. The cartoons were designed by Philippe de Champaigne and other 17th century French masters.

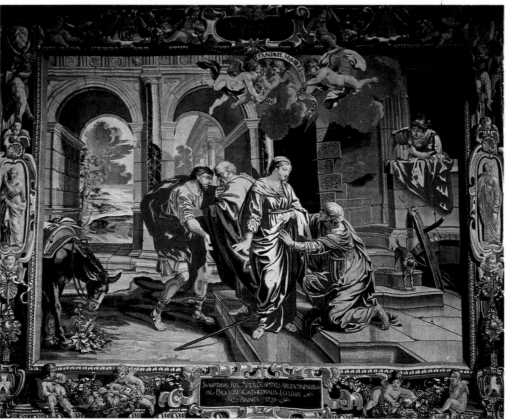

**Cathedral –
Two tapestries with scenes from
the life of the Virgin.**

Two picturesque views of the Cathedral buttressing and Rue Mercière from the top of the Cathedral.

Two more views of the Cathedral neighborhood taken from the top of the Cathedral. ▶

Cathedral Square with the Pharmacy of the Deer (left) and Kammerzell House (right, background).

# THE PHARMACY OF THE DEER

Located in Place de la Cathedrale in the heart of town, the Pharmacy of the Deer is one of the oldest in Europe. Amongst its celebrated clients was Goethe, who lived nearby on Rue du Viex-Marché-aus-Poissons and who often dropped in for a chat with his friend, the pharmacist Spielmann. Already documented in 1262, the pharmacy was rebuilt in the 15th century. The stone ground floor, covered by pointed-arch vaulting and decorated with sculpted foliage motifs, is a fine example of the 15th century late Gothic style. The upper floors, sporting typ-ical Alsatian exposed beam exteriors, were completed in 1567.

# KAMMERZELL HOUSE

This impressive wooden mansion with its distinctive slanted roof is one of the most picturesque dwellings on Cathedral Square. An earlier, 15th century, structure (of which only the stone ground floor is still extant) was purchased by a wealthy merchant. Martin Braun, in 1571. Braun commissioned the building of the upper stories which he had decorated with elaborate *wood carvings* of the signs of the zodiac, the five senses, the ages of man, and the heroes of mythology and medieval legends (the latter's popularity in the North lasted right through the Renaissance).

Over the years, despite the fact that it changed hands several times, the building's mercantile function never ceased. In fact, on the west side you can still see the winch which served to hoist the goods to and from the warehouse. In 1879 a grocer, M. Kammerzell, sold it to the Cathedral Board of Directors, who had it restored in 1892. Unfortunately, at this time the exterior was radically altered by the addition of murals attempting to imitate the style of the 16th century Renan artists.

The interior, which for many years has been a restaurant serv-

The picturesque Place Marché aux Cochons de Lait.

## PLACE MARCHE-AUX-COCHONS-DE-LAIT

ing delicacies of the local cuisine, was frescoed by Leo Schnugg. The subject of Schnugg's painting is a famous event in Strasbourg history, quite in keeping with restaurants. The story goes that in 1576, after an eighteen hour sail, a ship from Zurich docked at the riverport, bearing as a gift to the people of Strasbourg a pot of still-warm soup. This was done to prove to the allies of Zurich that when they needed help they would get it fast. Fragments of the historic pot are still preserved in the Museum of History.

Once the marketplace where piglets were bought and sold, this delightful square has preserved its 17th-18th century appearance intact. The finest of its quaint old buildings, No. 1, sports the exposed beams typical of Alsatian architecture.

The use of exterior galleries, however, is an interesting feature, since these were very popu-

lar in the country homes of the region, but are rarely found in town dwellings. The upper floor, built in 1617 over the stone ground floor, which is a good two centuries older, still belongs to the "golden period" of Strasbourg wooden architecture whose peak was reached in the late 1500s.

The boot-shaped flag-pole on the rooftop recalls a charming local legend. In 1415, the Emperor Sigismund was invited by the ladies of Strasbourg to attend a ball, but after trekking through the deep snow, he reached his

Nighttime view of the Place Marché aux Cochons de Lait. ▶

destination practically in tatters. The good ladies, feeling sorry for him, rushed out and bought him a pair of sturdy boots from the shoemaker whose shop was, as you might guess, at No. 1 Place Marché-aux-Cochons-de-Lait.

# THE CHATEAU ROHAN

Château Rohan, the fabulous residence of the bishops of Strasbourg was erected between 1731 and 1742. It was commissioned by Armand-Gaston de Rohan-Soubise, whose family had produced an entire century (the 18th) of Strasbourg's bishops and whose titles included Langrave of Lower Alsace and Imperial Prince.

The imposing complex, designed by Robert de Cotte, is composed of a group of buildings set around a square courtyard with four huge Corinthian columns in the center. The main façade looks out on the River Ill, while the north one — actually two pavillions joined by a portal carved with *allegorical statues* by Robert de Lorrain — faces out on the Place du Château. From the courtyard a staircase leads to the sumptuous reception suite ("*le Grand Appartement*"), inspired by Versailles' Baroque grandeur, and the more comfortable rooms ("*le Petit Appartement*") in the lighter Rococo style where the family actually lived. A curious note is to be found in one of the boudoirs. The nymphs in a Gobelins tapestry depicting the *Judgment of Paris* are prudishly depicted wearing dressing gowns in keeping with the taste of Mme de Maintenon, Louis XV's favorite, who thought it disgraceful to show off attractive nude bodies.

One of the many famous guests over the years was King Louis XV himself, who accompanied by his wife, Maria Leczinska, spent a period of convalescence in the castle. Great festivities were organized for the occasion and the buildings in front of the castle were hidden from view by a huge trompe-l'oeil canvas of a landscape in perspective. Another illustrious guest was Marie-Antoniette, who briefly sojourned here in 1770 before she became queen of France. Napoleon, who had been given the castle as a gift from the city of Strasbourg, also paid a visit in 1805.

Seriously damaged by bombs in 1944, the castle was totally restored and is presently occupied by the *Musée de Beaux-Arts,* the *Musée Archéologique,* and the *Musée des Arts Décoratifs.* The Musée de Beaux-Arts, on the second and third floors, contains 14th to 19th century Dutch, Flemish, Italian and Spanish paintings and an interesting collection of still-lifes. The Musée des Arts Décoratifs boasts one of the most celebrated collections of maiolica and porcelain in the world and, in addition, exhibits extensive documentation on the local crafts of Hannong and Haguenau.

The picturesque façade of the Cathedral Museum.

# THE CATHEDRAL MUSEUM

Housed inside a complex of buildings dating from the 14th through 17th centuries, the museum contains an assorted collection of works, most of which once belonged either to the cathedral or local and regional ecclesiastical buildings. The sculpture, paintings, stained glass, furnishings and jewelery on display enable the visitor to form a good idea of what Alsatian art was like throughout the Romanesque, Gothic, and Renaissance periods. Among the highlights of the collection are the originals of the cathedral's finest statues, a series of drawings and plans relating to the cathedral during its centuries-long construction, as well as paintings by Hans Baldung Grien and Konrad Witz (who executed an *altarpiece with Sts. Mary Magdalene and Catherine* especially for the city of Strasbourg).

# THE MUSEUM OF MODERN ART

Opened in 1965, the Museum of Modern Art occupies what was originally the customs house. Built in 1358, and enlarged in the 16th and 18th centuries, the original building had to be rebuilt after the war when it was practically totally destroyed.

All of the major artistic movements of the last 100 years are represented in the collection. There are paintings by Impressionist masters such as Monet, Pissarro, Renoir, Degas, and Boudin, watercolors and drawings by Gauguin, watercolors by Dufy and Paul Klee, and a still-life by Braque, famous for being the first Cubist painting shown in a French public collection. One of the best-known works in the museum is *The Kiss,* a huge preparatory study for a painting from the Stoclet Home in Brussels which Klimt, the Austrian master, was decorat-

The Museum of Modern Art: The side of the old Customs House along the river.

**The Museum of Modern Art: The façade viewed from the river.**

The river with the Museum of Modern Art (left) and the Museum of History (right).

ing c. 1910. A whole room is devoted to numerous plans and drawings by a native son of Strasbourg, the architect-artist Jean Arp (1877-1966), who was a member of the Blau Reuter group and one of the founders of the Dada movement.

A collection of 19th and 20th century stained glass documents the recent developments in a technique which for centuries has ranked as a major Strasbourg craft.

# THE MUSEUM OF HISTORY

This museum, like many others in Strasbourg, is situated in an historic building. Known as "La Grande Boucherie," it was built in 1587 and until 1859 served as the city's slaughterhouse and meat market.

Its varied collections illustrate the fascinating story of the city's past, including the political, eco-

nomic, military, and topographic highlights of medieval, Renaissance and Baroque Strasbourg. One of the most interesting displays is a 1:600 scale model of the city and its environs, built in 1727, and full of charming details. The military section is also extremely interesting, with its mementos of the French Revolution and the Napoleonic Em-

42

Detail of the
Museum of History ▶

pire — the periods of great ferment in Strasbourg history — as well as a unique collection of two hundred versions of Alsace uniforms from 1780 to 1940.

Exterior of the Cour du Corbeau.

# THE COUR DU CORBEAU

This quaint old inn, built in 1528 and open for business until 1854, is situated at no. 1 Quai des Bateliers, which, starting from the Middle Ages, was where the local fishermen and boatmen made their homes. Its less than elegant address, however, failed to keep away the rich and famous. Among the guests of the Cour du Corbeau were Marshall Turenne, the philosopher Voltaire, and even royalty such as Frederick the Great of Prussia and the Emperor Joseph II of Austria, who made his stay incognito. An uninspiring façade, the result of a 19th century restoration, hides the magnificent courtyard around which are the 16th and 17th all-wood build-

The Cour du Corbeau: the interior.

ings that make up the inn. According to a popular tradition, the wood balconies running around the building were specially treated with a potion of ox blood from the nearby Grande Boucherie to ensure their perfect preservation. Of note are the courtyard's architectural details, such as the covered galleries with lead windows connecting the sides of the courtyard, and the octagonal turret inside of which is a winding staircase leading to the upper floors.

**Two views of the interior of the picturesque Cour du Corbeau.**

The inner courtyard of the Museum of Alsace.

# THE MUSEUM OF ALSACE

In a region such as Alsace which has a deeply-ingrained sense of the past and deep-rooted attachment to the rural traditions of long ago, it is hardly surprising to find a museum such as the Museum and Arts and Folk Traditions.

The collections are displayed inside three picturesque houses, which are not only museum buildings, but are themselves fascinating mementos of Strasbourg's past. The exhibits cover furnishings, pottery, artifacts, and native costumes worn by the peasants of the region. Interiors of 17th through 19th century city and country dwellings have been accurately reconstructed, giving the visitor a sense of the quiet home-centered lives once led by the Alsatians. Other rooms document the agriculture of the region, especially wine producing, Alsace's main economic resource, and another section is devoted to illustrating traditional arts and crafts.

# PLACE GUTENBERG

Known until 1781 as Marché-aux-Herbes (Vegetable Market), this square was the city's economic-administrative hub from the Middle Ages up to the French Revolution, and the site of celebrations marking the main events of Alsatian life. Two of the most famous are the festivities held for the birth of the Duke of Bourgogne in 1682 and those for the visit of King Louis XVI in 1744, when fountains abundantly spurting the best Alsatian wines were set up in the square. The present – day Chamber of Commerce building, completed in 1585, was erected to house the trade associations (ground floor) and city government offices (upper floors). The competition for the construction of the building, called in 1580, established that it should be the stateliest in Strasbourg. The winning design, quite unlike the traditional Gothic-style wood architecture of Alsace, was inspired by the Italian Renaissance style which exerted great influence throughout France during the late 16th century. The result is a curious mixture: the rusticated stone arches of the ground floor, the portal surmounted by a bust of Hermes (patron of commerce), and the Ionic and Corinthian pilaster strips of the upper floors are Classical and Renaissance, while the skylighted slanted roof adds a strictly Northern touch of fantasy.

General view of the Place Gutenberg with the monument to Gutenberg in the middle.

# MONUMENT TO GUTENBERG

The stately bronze statue of the great inventor who lived in Strasbourg from 1433 to 1445 was executed by David d'Angers in 1840 to commemorate the fourth centennial of the invention of the printing press. In fact, it was here in Strasbourg that Gutenberg's invention first saw the light.

Gutenberg, however, did not work alone — he was aided by a goldsmith and a carpenter who fashioned the metal type without which the press could not function.

Although the second and third centennials were marked by solemn celebrations, the people of Strasbourg wanted something even more memorable for the fourth, so they commissioned d'Angers, a friend of the famous writer, Victor Hugo, to sculpt a commemorative statue. The sculpture depicts Gutenberg standing by his press showing a page printed with the Old Testament verse "*Et la lumière fut...*" ("and there was light"). The four bronze reliefs on the base, also by d'Angers, illustrate the benefits that Gutenberg's invention has brought to mankind.

◀ **Two views of Place Gutenberg.**

**The Monument to Gutenberg.** ▶

# PLACE DE L'HOMME-DE-FER

Little of the original charm of this square, known during the Middle Ages as the Square of the Lime Trees, is extant today. Destroyed by bombs during World War II, the old buildings have since been replaced by lackluster structures erected in the 1950s and a soaring tower, hardly in keeping with the Gothic spire of the nearby cathedral. Nevertheless, the 18th century building — after which the present-day square was named — at no. 2, is still intact. In 1740 no. 2 was a gunsmith's shop whose street sign was an iron man (homme-de-fer) i.e. a life-size mannequin of a sergeant of the municipal guard dressed in 16th century armor. In 1870 when the gunsmith's shop was closed and the pharmacy, still in business, took over the premises, the original iron man was put on display in the medieval section of the Museum of History and a copy was put up in its place.

**Place de l'Homme-de-Fer and a detail of the statue.**

# PLACE KLEBER
# AND MONUMENT

This square is one of the places most loved by the citizens of Strasbourg. Here the military parades of the Ancien Régime were held, here the events of the French Revolution were marked, and here, twice, the end of a world war was joyously celebrated. In fact, due to its long association with military events, the people of Strasbourg chose it as the burial place for Napoleon's celebrated hero and native of Strasbourg. General Kléber whose mortal remains were to perpetually rest beneath the bronze commemorative statue in the middle of the square sculpted by Philippe Grass in 1840. The people of the city wished to give honorable burial to the great soldier, who had perished in the Egyptian campaign of 1800, and who was a symbol of Strasbourg's ties to France. Unhappily, in 1940, the Nazis arrogantly removed the statue and buried the urn with Kléber's ashes in the Military Cemetery of Cronenbourg. Finally in 1945, the statue of General Kléber, together with *commemorative reliefs of the battles of Altenkirchen and Heliopolis,* was restored to its rightful place in the square named after him, where it has been standing ever since.

**Two views of Place Kléber.**

Two views of the charming neighborhood called « Petite France ».

◀ On the preceding page: a view of the Covered Bridges with two of the three towers.

# THE COVERED BRIDGES AND LA "PETITE FRANCE"

In the 13th century, numerous wooden bridges with sturdy watch-towers flanking them were built over branches of the River Ill to defend the city from attack. In the 16th century, slanted roofs were added as further protection. The bridges were extant until 1784 (The present stone structures were built between 1860 and 1870.) Now all that remains of the famous covered bridges is their name.

Fortunately, however, three of the imposing medieval towers (the *Hangman's Tower,* the *French Tower,* and the *Tower of Chains*) have survived. On the third floor of the Hangman's Tower you can still see the tiny cells where the condemned, awaiting their unhappy fate, scrawled names and other messages on the walls.

The French Tower, which rises on the islet in the middle, was also called "la Petite France" recalling the time when François I's French troops roamed the area in search of adventure. The chains of the third tower are believed to refer to those used to secure the prisoners locked inside before being embarked for transfer.

One of the houses by Pont Saint-Martin.

## THE TANNERS' DISTRICT AND RUE DU BAIN-AUX-PLANTES

Although Rue du Bain-aux-Plantes, once one of the most picturesque streets in the city, has not been spared the "improvements" of the modern era, it still contains several 16th and 17th century buildings worthy of note. Most of these have to do with the tanners who once occupied an important position in the city's economy and lived and worked in this neighborhood.

The hides used to be laid out to dry on the roofs and open galleries along the façades of these buildings, which practically all ceased to function in the 19th century when leather-tanning lost its economic importance. Originally, the buildings were completely surrounded by tannin plants which, when full-grown, were cut and laid upon special mats made of rushes to dry in the sun. The tannin was thus transformed into the cheap and plentiful source of fuel known as "lohkas" which the tanners could not do without. And, in fact, Lohkas is the name of the tanners' favorite tavern, a late 16th century wood and stone building, still extant at no. 25 Rue du Bain-aux-Plantes.

The building at no. 42, known as Tanner's House, was built around the same time in a similar style. Its unusual façade of superimposed galleries overlooks the Ill.

The Maison des Tanneurs, one of the loveliest buildings in the Tanners' District.

The Church of Saint-Paul in a nighttime view taken from the Ill River.

# THE CHURCH OF SAINT-PAUL

The church is located in the district of Strasbourg known as German Town. Built after Alsace-Lorraine was ceded to the German Empire in 1870, the district was designed to be the new political-administrative center of the city and as such was endowed with imposing public buildings and criss-crossed by a geometric network of avenues. The architects, Orth and Conrath, were evidently very much influenced by the eclectic style popular at the turn of the century: the Palais du Rhin, for example, the huge building that dominates Place de la Republique, was inspired by similar imitation Renaissance buildings buildings then being built in Berlin, as was the Palais de l'Université, which rises on the square of the same name. On the other hand, the Protestant church, l'Eglise de Saint-Paul, beautifully situated on the green banks of the Ill, was erected in the neo-Gothic style in 1892 (the church of St. Elizabeth in Marburg served as its model).

View of the Church of Saint-Paul. ▶

# THE PALAIS DE L'EUROPE

Right after the war, the major Western European nations decided it was time to set up a united European organization, and immediately picked Strasbourg as its headquarters (although the designation became official only in 1949).
In 1950, when Strasbourg, under the dynamic leadership of mayor M. Charles Frey, was still deeply involved in postwar reconstruction, the first European

The interior of the Palais de l'Europe.

◀ Two views of the ultramodern Palais de l'Europe.

Council buildings started to rise on a $12^1/_2$ acre plot, a park known as l'Orangerie, which had been partially designed by La Nôtre, the landscape architect of Versailles.

This was followed by the *Palais des Droits de l'Homme* (Palace of Human Rights), designed by B. Monnet as a simple horizontal building with geometric accents (inspired by Le Corbusier's Harvard Center in Cambridge, Massachusetts), built in 1964 on the nearby Place du President Schumann.

The most recent building of the new Strasbourg international center is the Palais de l'Europe designed by Henry Bernard and completed in 1967. This gigantic complex, built to house the Council's huge Hall of Parliament and its numerous offices, is a deliberate break with much of contemporary architecture.

On the outside, the great square-shaped building pierced by dozens of slit-like windows interspersed with pincer-shaped buttresses looks like some kind of futuristic fortress. On the inside is the Hall of Parliament, spanned by an immense transparent dome, where the representatives elected for the first time in 1979 by the citizens of the nine countries of the Common Market, hold their meeting and debates.

# THE PALAIS DU RHIN

The hub of "German Town," built after Strasbourg was annexed to the German Empire in 1870, is Place de la Republique, originally known as Kaiser Platz. The square is wholly dominated by the imposing Imperial Palace designed by Hermann Heggert between 1883 and 1889 in imitation of the public buildings in Berlin, which, in turn, were eclectic versions of Florentine Renaissance palaces. In the center of the main façade (the rusticated stone facing is a typical Florentine hallmark), is a protruding balcony shaped like the frontal of a Classical temple. The whole is surmount-

Sunset over the twin towers of the Covered Bridges.

◀ The Palais du Rhin, with a detail of its Classical-style architecture.

ed by a huge dome covering a grandiose hall with a monumental staircase leading up to the second floor ballroom and royal apartments (unfortunately most of their furnishings perished in the 1944 bombings). When Alsace-Lorraine was restored to France in 1918, the building was given its present name, Palais du Rhin, and is now the headquarters for the Department of Cultural Affairs.

On the north side of the square is another impressive building. Erected in the imperial period as the Ministry of Alsace-Lorraine and presently the headquarters of the préfecture, it imitates German Baroque architecture of 1720-1740, whose foremost monument is the sumptuous Bishops' Palace in Wurzburg.

The so-called "German Town" was deliberately built in an area separate from the rest of the city for the purpose of emphasizing the special German cultural imprint imposed upon the recently-annexed territory. Yet today, due to the postwar building boom, it perfectly fits into the eclectic urbanistic context of the modern-day city of Strasbourg.

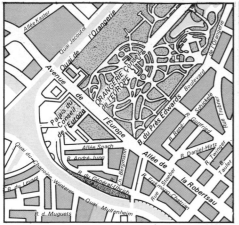

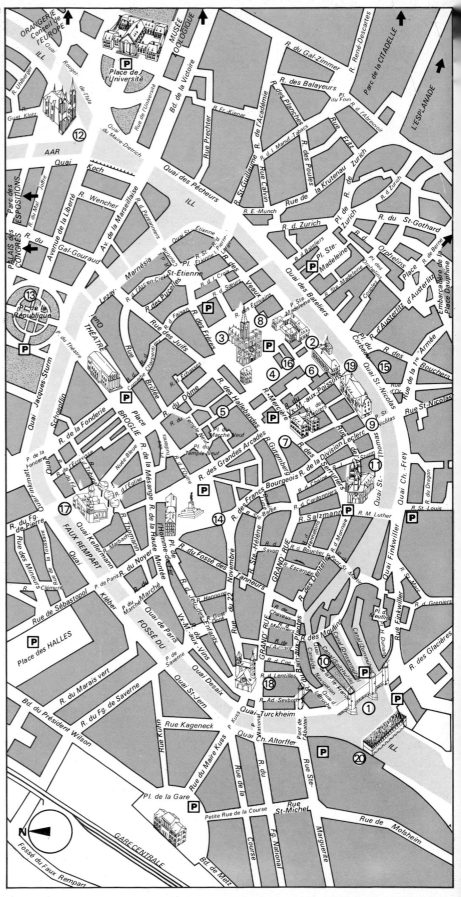

1 Covered bridges
2 Place Marché-aux-Cochons-de-Lait
3 Cathedral
4 Kammerzell House
5 Rue des Orfèvres
6 Museum of History
7 Place Gutenberg
8 Château Rohan
9 Old Customs House (Museum of Modern Art)
10 "Petite France"
11 Church of Saint-Thomas
12 Church of Saint-Paul
13 Place de la République
14 Place Kléber
15 Museum of Alsace
16 Little Cathedral Museum
17 Church of Saint Peter the Young
18 Church of Saint Peter the Old
19 Cour de Corbeau
20 Barrage Vauban